su·per·hu·man

adjective

1. above or beyond what is human; having a higher nature or greater powers than humans have: a superhuman being.

2. exceeding ordinary human power, achievement, experience, etc.: a superhuman effort.

Webster's College Dictionary,
© Random House

1

Contents

1. Introduction

"When your desires are strong enough, you will appear to possess superhuman powers to achieve."
Napoleon Hill – 20th Century American Self-Help Author

At the age of 56 years, Brian Blessed climbed higher up Everest than any other person of his age had before him. At the ages of 7 and 8, Venus and Serena Williams were up and hitting tennis balls at 6am, and went on to win over 40 singles and doubles Grand Slam titles between them. At the age of 59 Tom Watson led much of the 2009 Open Championship in golf, 26 years after his last Major victory. At the age of 17 Stephen Hawking went to Oxford University, and later to Cambridge, and despite developing a motor neuron disorder went on to become a brilliant, theoretical physicist. At the age of 26 Albert Einstein published a scientific theory that revolutionized physics having not talked until the age of 3. At the age of 42 Rosa Parks refused to give up her seat on a bus to a white man and became the mother of the freedom movement. At the age of 79 Mohandas Gandhi, the father of an Independent India, fasted to stop wide-spread violence in his country. At the age of 39 comedian Ellen DeGeneres came out as a high-profile, gay, public figure, and is a strong activist for their cause. At the age of 44 Nelson Mandela was convicted of sabotage and conspiracy to overthrow the Government and spent 27 years in prison before being released, at the age of 71, later becoming President of South Africa. At the age of 74 Clint Eastwood won a Best Director Oscar for Million Dollar Baby after a lifetime of working in films. At the age of 10 Tatum O'Neal won a Best Actress in a Supporting Role Oscar for her performance in Paper Moon, the youngest ever to receive the award. At the age of 17 Boris Becker is the youngest person ever to have won the men's singles title at Wimbledon. At the age of 20 Hannah Cockcroft, who started wheelchair racing when she was at university, won gold in the 100m and 200m events at the London 2012 Paralympics, beating previous Paralympic records. At the age of 23, overcoming racial prejudices against him, Jessie Owens won 4 gold medals at the Berlin 1936 Olympics, where he was its most successful athlete.

The point is that these are all people like you or I, it doesn't matter what age you are, what gender, what race or sexuality, able-bodied or disabled, you have the potential to be Superhuman, to accomplish incredible feats, to be able to do more than you think you can do, help others and yourself to succeed. Greatness lies inside of you.

Being Superhuman is a choice. It's a way of living and believing in yourself, believing what you can achieve and acting upon it. The intention of this book is to help you do that by unleashing the awesome power inside of you. You can be the most outstanding version of yourself and live a good and happy life.

The change to being Superhuman can happen at any time in your life, so why not now? This is the moment that you decide to act, this is the time for you to show your true brilliance, this is when your life starts anew.

Superhumans walk among us. You could be one of them. You could rank among their number.

Superhuman You.

Write down what it is you want to get from reading this book:

2. Beginnings

"A journey of a thousand miles begins with a single step."
Lao Tzu – Ancient Chinese Philosopher

Your first step was in buying this book, or reading the first few pages online, or anywhere else that you found it. Either way, your journey has begun; you've taken your first step.

I like reading self-improvement books, and one that I read had questions in it and spaces where you could write responses. The book became a more interactive experience and I felt greater engagement in the process. So, for this book I decided to use a similar technique. At the end of each chapter there is an inquiry relevant to the chapter content for you to put a response.

I saw how powerful a form of collaboration it was for myself when I wrote about the character attributes that I wanted. Just considering those qualities and recognising they were traits I sought made me feel more of those words and they were what I became.

I've not used any of the words in this chapter because it is important that you develop your own list of words from what you want or need to be more of a Superhuman You. These are the words that will form your character, deeply imbedded and impermeable in your mind. They are what you will become.

Another book I read had in it inspiring quotes from various renowned people. Learning from the wisdom of the experienced and astute is a Superhuman You quality so I have included quotes at the beginning of each chapter, again relevant to the chapter content. Each one is intended to be a succinct, thought provoking, stimulating idea to start the chapter with, and it indicates what the chapter will be about.

Make a list of the character attributes that you would like to say that you are:

3. The Tomorrow List

"The secret of getting things done is to act."
Dante Alighieri – Medieval Italian Poet

I have used many different versions of "To Do" lists beginning from when I was at college. Some lasted several months, others a few days. I reached a time when I didn't like the process anymore and stopped using them.

Then, when I had been unwell for a while and didn't do much each day and wanted to do more, I had an idea. I realised the only time that you can really plan to affect is tomorrow. You can decide what you want to do the next day, and then do it when it is *today*.

I took a piece of lined A4 paper and I folded it horizontally in half, then vertically, then horizontally, and I was left with a section of the page of around 7 or 8 lines. At the top I wrote "Tomorrow List 1." Then I wrote a list of activities I wanted to get done the next day.

Some were reminders of daily tasks such as "brush" (my teeth), "ex × 2" (the daily exercises and ½ an hour workout that I do), and "read" (also for ½ an hour each day).

Some were lessons I had for tuition so I just wrote their names, "Paul" and "Jennifer" for example, or there was a reminder for an appointment, such as "dentist" or "osteopath." Others were household tasks I needed to do, such as "iron", "wash/ dry" (clothes) and "dishes."

Then it is a case of ticking them when they are completed. At the end of a day you award yourself one smiley face if you have completed some of the tasks, and two if you complete all of them. It is positive reinforcement that you give yourself.

The folded piece of lined A4 paper has 8 sections on it, so that's 6 days of the week Monday to Saturday, and I leave Sunday blank to have a day off. In the bottom right section I put a title "Weekly Aims" so the mid–term is thought about as well and some of the daily activities need to relate and build up to them. Examples of "Weekly Aims" would be "improve fitness", "socialize more" and "get better results at work."

I began using the List whilst I was working part-time, if you are working full-time then most of the items during the week may relate to what you need to get done at your place of employment. It could be that you only write a List on Saturday or Sunday or perhaps it can be used for the mornings and evenings before and after work: it's flexible for however you want to use it. When you have done a week on the front you can do a week on the back, then on a new piece of folded paper, at the top, you write "Tomorrow List 2."

I like it because it's a reminder for all that I want to get done each day. It's a motivator and a check-off reference guide. It keeps you using time well, being efficient and maintaining the repetition of tasks that you need to do daily. I highly recommend it for you to get the same benefits too.

Another organisational tool I use is the display of the month's calendar on my mobile phone. You can input what day and time different events are occurring. It reminds you when you have various appointments and activities. An alarm can be set as well to tell you ½ an hour before you need to be there. It means that you will always remember all that is important.

By whatever means a Superhuman You is focused, organised and on top of all that you need to accomplish, then you can complete what you have to do and still have time left over for what you want to do. You can achieve great results, plan ahead and remember and do everything in your day.

Mark down a day's worth of activities of all that you would like to get done:

4. Courageous You

"Life expands in proportion to one's courage."
Anaïs Nin – 20th Century French Author

When I was growing up I developed a concern about spiders. One day my friend suggested taking a fairly small spider to show his mum. We did and she was surprised and hit her head on a clothes-hanging frame in their back garden. Seeing her reaction at a young age I saw that as an appropriate response: it was learnt behaviour.

I went on to be unsure of them. When I was at college I realised why I had the trepidation and decided I didn't want it anymore. I first of all found small money spiders and let them run around on my hands. They were so tiny they were effortless and fine to handle. Then I moved onto zebra spiders, still quite small, and as their name suggests they are black and white. What I really liked about them was that they could hop.

Next I sought out garden spiders, which often sit in the centre of their webs, and they have a mottled mid and dark brown colouration. The size had increased to medium and over a few months I was building up my courage.

Then there were harvest spiders that have a small body and long thin legs, by the time I reached this stage they were easy to hold. I was de-sensitising myself to the stimulus.

The last step was the best. I found house spiders and caught them with a pint glass and piece of white card. I would turn the glass the right way up, so the spider fell to the bottom, put my hand over the top of the glass, then turned it upside down again. The spider was still trapped inside but it was on my hand. They were big spiders and it took firm resolve but I did it because I wanted to overcome any concerns and recondition myself.

I found spiders around the house and was eager to take on the glass challenge many times. Then finally I had the spider on my hand, taking the glass away, so it was free to walk around. I had become so bold I could let it walk from hand to hand.

Mission achieved: I had triumphed over the circumstances. And it's one possible technique to do it in developmental stages, so you build up your courage and expand your comfort zone gradually, being in control at every stage.

When I was at college I had an issue with answering questions in front of the class. I was not as courageous as I wanted to be. This was most true of my A-Level English Literature class where often you were giving your own opinion. I didn't accept being unable to contribute and wanted to change it, I wanted to be secure and say whatever I liked.

I had the idea of thinking the same phrase over and over in my head, "I am strong. I am strong." for several months whenever I wanted to give a response to a question in front of the class.

There were a number of occasions that I developed and changed. One time I thought, "I am strong" and then, automatically, "I know I am. Why wouldn't I be?" which was really great.

Another time I made a comment and followed up with another after the teacher spoke. A fellow student on my right said to me, "That was out of character." Awesome. Sometimes then I gave my opinion and answers to the class and I was robust as I had thought myself into being brave, I had overcome the circumstances.

Later I went on to teach and would be talking in front of groups of about twenty to thirty pupils, all the school day, every weekday. I was the centre of attention and happy to be so, and making other people more secure about answering questions in front of a class by being positive and friendly. I was a self-assured person in that setting, a massive change from how I used to be.

My greatest successes have been in how I interact with people. Concerns arose from some events in my childhood, but it doesn't really matter, what matters is how you respond. Whatever the situation is you have to surmount it. You just have to want it. You have to want it more than all that is in the way of it. You overcome the issue and move on, and it becomes as if it was never even there in the first place.

You can work out steps to build your courage and find a way to get where you want to be, as Ruth Gordon, the 20th century American actress said, "Courage is like a muscle; it is strengthened by use." Force of will, determination and understanding will make anything possible.

There is a gap between stimulus and response. As a Superhuman You you stand in that gap and decide how you want to react. Courage wins over everything else. You fight for what you want, what's right and what you believe in, for the good of others and yourself.

Your conscious and sub-conscious minds have to be united towards success. The concern only exists in your head, and therefore can be vanquished and only you may know how heroic you've been: the mental battles you have fought and won, your Superhuman You cape flapping in the breeze behind you.

Note times when you have been courageous, strong and overcome your uncertainties:

5. Mission Statement

"Personal mission statements are like a personal constitution, the basis for making major, life-directing decisions."
Stephen R. Covey – 20th and 21st Century American Educator, Management Specialist and Author

It is important to know where your life is headed and what you want it to be about. What you focus on is what you get. So focus on the right aspects, those actions and activities that matter to you and are the most beneficial to your life and others.

A personal mission statement will do that for you. It could be written and substantial but is more probable to be a few sentences long. I like brevity and being succinct so mine was only 3 sentences, including what I desired my values, achievements and behaviour to include. Later I reduced the 3 sentences to 6 words, 3 concepts of 2 words each that embodied the ambitions for my life. With simplicity each word carries more weight, and will mean more to you. Later still I changed it to a single sentence to really focus on what I wanted and what I needed to do to get it.

A mission statement gives you more direction and purpose. It forms a part of your long-term goals and focuses the daily tasks and weekly aims towards your ultimate ambitions.

A Superhuman You recognises the worth of having a life plan which will define your actions, decide your guiding mindset and will give you ambitions to believe in and aim for. The words that you choose, the sentences that you construct, the ideas and thoughts within your personal mission statement are a manifestation of you and your values, it sets out your intentions and leads toward the outcomes in your life.

Use the space below to write a first draft of a personal mission statement for yourself:

6. Food and Drink

"A healthy outside starts from the inside."
Robert Ulrich – 20th and 21st Century American
Film, Television and Stage Actor

Eating is a crucial part of the relationship between you and your body, as with drinking as well. I think that it's vital to eat healthily but at the same time to take pleasure in what you eat.

My eating habits have changed and improved throughout my life and it is a route worth taking. As I became an adult, I began to savour various fruit and vegetables more. Partly I sampled different foods with an open mind, I experimented and found what I liked and I actively changed my preferences.

With fruit I've always relished different varieties of apples and pears, but even then, it's a case of finding those that you value most. I thought that oranges were unwieldy to eat unless they were cut into segments but I tried satsumas and clementines and they were made up of mouth-sized pieces, were very easy to eat, and tasted great. They became firm favourites.

The other main fruit to eat is the banana. I didn't appreciate their taste but I wanted to be able to eat them as they were another healthy food. I set myself to changing my tastes. The first banana I ate made me feel unwell, but each one I ate after that, over a few weeks, became nicer and nicer, and it took until the eighth one before I fully appreciated it. From then I have enjoyed eating bananas, so you can change what you like.

I have a piece of fruit every day and my weekly shop keeps me stocked up for it. It's good to eat them when they are ripe so you get the best taste possible.

I increased the number of vegetables I ate as well. You can have them with dinner, items such as potatoes, carrots, peas, beans or mushrooms. I keep stocked up with tomatoes, green peppers and round lettuce too. They go with many different meals. I really like a bought pasta sauce, penne pasta, round lettuce with chopped up green pepper, tomato and salami, or those last 3 ingredients in an omelette. You can also have vegetables with sandwiches: tuna or prawns and lettuce; cheese and tomato; bacon, lettuce and tomato; or soft cheese and cumber; most with margarine or butter.

There are so many fruits and vegetables to try. Eat and find what you are partial to. Takeaways too can be good, but at most once a week. My family has a rotor of takeaways that we have together weekly. Variety and infrequency work well.

It's beneficial to have a good breakfast, and later a proper lunch and then a full dinner with no snacks in-between. If your portion sizes are too big then buy smaller plates to reduce how much you have. Smaller meals will shrink the size of your stomach. Eat well, as much as you need, no more, to help stay healthy.

I only drink tap water with meals. Rinse the glass out properly before filling it to make sure it

19

tastes good. Then, as it hasn't been flavoured by a concentrated juice, it doesn't interfere with the flavours of your meal. Milk is also good to drink sometimes, or with a bowl of cereal for breakfast, or to make pancakes, and pure orange or apple juice can be good as well, maybe after breakfast.

A Superhuman You can make sensible choices and understands that the food and drink you put into yourself affects what you get out. The best consumables for you are the natural ones, made to make you healthy.

Record what healthy foods, drinks and meals you would enjoy incorporating into your diet:

7. Exercise for Fun

"Motivation is what gets you started; habit is what keeps you going."
Jim Ryun – 20th and 21st Century American Track Athlete and Politician

I had M.E. and later M.S. and for this I was given the advice to pace, plan and prioritise what I did and not do too much each day. It maintained a feeling of being okay but I wanted more for myself than that. I wanted to be fit, strong and healthy.

So I bought an X-Box 360 with Kinect and I bought a game called "Kinect Sports." You are the controller, so you have to move around to play the different activities. I gradually built up from playing 5 minutes a day to 10, then 15 and so on until, over a few months, I built up to doing 30 minutes a day, later going back down to 20 because I felt that was all I needed.

It became a part of my daily routine. I would do it in the morning a while after breakfast. And the great part was I enjoyed playing the sports of Football, Bowling, Table Tennis, Beach Volleyball, Boxing and Athletics.

In Football you have to do kicking motions to pass the ball and shoot with it, and use your arms to save shots from the other team. It's excellent in improving your balance and you can use both legs to give each of them a workout.

In Bowling it is the swinging of either arm to bowl a ball and knock down pins, using muscles in your arms and upper body.

In Table Tennis you have a swinging motion and a greater lateral turn of your back to serve, return and hit smash shots, again using either arm.

In Beach Volleyball you jump to serve, spike and block the ball, and you set and dig it as well. It is an arm, leg and back workout, and more to test your balance with.

In Boxing there are different types of punch to use on your opponent to knock them out, and you can raise your guard to block punches.

In Athletics there are several events: 100 metres, 110 metre Hurdles, Long Jump, Javelin and Discuss. They require various skills and you running on the spot is a part of all of them except for the Discuss.

The sports entail varying levels of exercise. Bowling has a low amount; Table Tennis, Football and Beach Volleyball a medium amount; and Boxing and Athletics a high amount. And each one, apart from Bowling, the amount of energy you expend can be increased with a higher setting of achievement from Beginner to Amateur, to Professional to Champion.

After I had improved my fitness to a good standard, I had a lumbar puncture and that was a readjustment for me as I couldn't do any exercise for a while, but when I could I built myself back up again using "Kinect Sports." I gradually increased the amount I played each day and progressed through the levels of challenge.

Then the next year someone collided with the back of my car. I had to rest and recover, see an osteopath as well, for some injuries, but when I could I built myself back up once more using "Kinect Sports." It was my rehabilitation.

It works for me because it's convenient, it's in my own home, apart from the initial cost it's free and I revel in playing the sports so I am happy to do it long-term every day for 20 minutes.

Whatever exercise you enjoy doing most will be best for a Superhuman You. There are the team sports of Football, Netball, Volleyball, Hockey, Rugby, Basketball, Cricket and many others. And you can play anything from a knockabout with a few friends to a full competitive match. Then there are sports for 2 to 4, such as the racket sports Tennis, Squash, Badminton, Table Tennis; and more leisurely pursuits like Golf. Aside from those you can do jogging, going to a gym, yoga or Pilates classes, or whatever else there is on offer nearby. There is cycling as well, going for a walk: there are so many options for you to try. It is only important that you love it and that it is a good workout for you and you stay active.

I exercise for 20 minutes daily now because I am fortunate enough to have the time to do so. As long as you raise your heart rate for 15 minutes or longer, 3 times a week or more, then you will be making the Superhuman You fitter and healthier.

It helps your mindset, builds a more positive, stronger self-belief and because you're having fun it is of benefit to your general happiness.

Sport and exercise are to be enjoyed by you on your own or with your family, a friend, or friends. You can be a member of a team and even play in a league. Whatever level you want to take part in is fine, as a Superhuman You, you will find what you like and enjoy and gather the rewards wholeheartedly.

A healthy body is a Superhuman You body.

Make a plan of what exercise you want to do each day or a few times a week or on weekends:

8. Interdependent You

"All have their worth and each contributes to the worth of others."
J.R.R. Tolkien/ The Silmarillion – 20th Century English Author

To live dependently is to rely on the effort, work and good nature of others. Commonly people may have to do this when they are young, old or unwell. It involves statements that include "you" in them, such as "How can you help me?" "What are you doing to fix this?"

To live independently is to rely on yourself only. It is a step up from dependence as you can get activities done by yourself, for yourself and without the help of others. It involves statements with "I" in them, such as "I can work out how to do this." "I will sort this out." "I will decide what I want to do."

To live interdependently is to work with other people co-operatively to accomplish better results than you could by yourself. It involves statements that include "we" in them, such as "How can we work together to make it easier for both of us?" Or even "How can I help you?" and "How can you help me?"

It is the most effective way of living. Within it you help others and they help you and together as Aristotle, the ancient Greek philosopher and polymath, said, "The whole is greater than the sum of its parts." You can be more than what you are on your own, achieve more, be capable of more and harvest the advantages from working together.

When I had a lumbar puncture for my diagnosis of M.S. it had not a good affect on me, for a week afterwards I could barely walk and I had to spend all my time lying in bed or on the sofa. My mum made all my meals and drinks of water for me and during that period I was totally reliant. After that I required lifts to work from my dad, another dependent act. I was fortunate to have the support of my parents in a particular time of need.

Later, with continuing M.S. issues, a friend of mine brought around one or two left over meals each week. I was grateful for the food that I could heat up and didn't have to expend money, energy or time on.

Also my parents continued to be very supportive and visited once a week on Sundays to help me with housework and household jobs. They did what I found not too straightforward to do.

I in turn tried to be a good friend to the friend that helped me, and to be a good son to my parents. I help them with whatever they need and with whatever I can, whenever I can.

Working with others to benefit all of you is the ideal situation, and in a wider context, we live in a society where the desired premise is that we look after each other: the well support the unwell, the fortunate support the unfortunate. We live interdependent lives where our actions affect others and how other people behave affects our lives too. It's so easy and worthwhile to say "please" and "thank you" to someone, to smile at or be helpful to a stranger, be as you would wish people be to you, act as you would like people to act towards you.

If you live a good and a beneficial life you will be in a network of interrelatedness with a significant other, your friends, family, your work colleagues and society as a whole to the increased advantage of you all.

To be a Superhuman You, you first have to become an Interdependent You, do that and your life and the lives of those that you help will be made better for it.

Detail ways in which your endeavours, through your work or personal life, are interdependent:

9. Hero Worship

*"How important it is for us to recognize and
celebrate our heroes and she-roes!"*
*Maya Angelou – 20th and 21st Century American
Author and Poet*

It's good to have heroes: men and women that
you look up to. People that you admire for who
they are and what they have achieved can be
inspirational to you, a great motivating force as you
can see how they managed to get success in their
lives and, therefore, how you can with yours.

Heroes can be found in sport, TV, film and any
profession you have an interest in, like architecture,
engineering, music and painting; anyone that works
hard, has talent and is successful. It can include
fictional characters in books, TV and film as well as
they can have attributes that you aspire towards and
have great quotes written for them.

The main area where I find the greatest amount
of inspiration is with people involved in social
change; and people who work for equality either by
ethnicity, gender or sexuality using peaceful means.

As a Superhuman You you have to decide what
areas interest you, what values you want, whom you
desire to resemble and which people in what
occupations you most admire. It is great to have a
world full of so many wonderful people.

There are fantastic philanthropists of the modern
age and the Victorian age. There are amazing
inventors making beneficial contributions to

developing countries. There are inspiring athletes making huge sacrifices to achieve the highest honours in their sport. There are such talented people in the world of entertainment.

Then there are heroes in your own life: friends and family, work colleagues, someone that you are in a relationship with, someone you know; anyone that you admire and value.

There are heroes for everyone, more than enough for a Superhuman You.

Make a list of your own particular set of heroes and what you admire about them:

10. Solution Orientated

"There are no problems, only solutions."
John Lennon – 20th Century English Musician,
Singer and Songwriter

I see the world as being full of solutions. Sometimes you have to think carefully and creatively to find them but they are always there.

When you encounter a problem that is the approach to take: know that there is a solution and you have only to work it out. Other people can help you realize it, but the solutions that are most worthwhile to your life and endeavours are ones that you think of yourself.

I was too unwell to be a full-time classroom teacher so I became a part-time tutor and later a supply teacher as well. I worked in respect to my new abilities and enjoyed the change very much.

I had unease with not being mentally and physically energized so I exercised and read every day to improve my fitness and cerebral agility. I exercised and read more than before I had become unwell.

I had an issue with my left hand being unstill, so I learnt to be right-handed and then I was more in control. I could do everything that I could do before so long as I kept working out solutions.

I had an unsteady balance so that was a skill I practised whilst playing "Kinect Sports" and, as a part of my morning exercises that I created and developed through seeing a Physiotherapist, I tensed my core muscles to make them stronger and enabled my balance to be better.

I had speech issues so I saw a Vocal Therapist and learnt different techniques to help me be more communicative.

When I was really unwell with M.E. I went on a course called "The Lightning Process" created by Dr Phil Parker PhD, a 20th and 21st century osteopath, therapist and author. It is a form of Neuro-Linguistic Programming and explained a lot more of how the disorder worked, and gave me the tools I needed to conquer it: the mental processes to recondition my mind.

Later, when I was finding it not good with M.S. concerns, but before I knew what was the matter with me, I saw a hypnotherapist who was also trained in Neuro-Linguistic Programming, and Cognitive Behavioural Therapy. She was very well qualified and was excellent at what she did and she improved my outlook substantially.

I sought and found what I required to be well again, or to have a much better approach to the issues that I had, and it was as simple as a magazine article and a Google search to find the right people, but you have to try for it. Solutions don't often present themselves; you have to work for them, use your knowledge and experience or improve what you know by investigation, thoughtful endeavour and wise jumps in solution-making.

A Superhuman You looks for and finds solutions to challenges whenever they are encountered. It may be that you seek out other people's help but usually the solutions lie inside of you. You are more perceptive and wiser than you know. Trust in your ability to be your own greatest supporter and get what you need done. Be brave and persistent so that the solutions you find, and commit yourself to act on fully, will improve your life. Solutions are out there for a Superhuman You and they are there for the taking. Every situation has one, as a challenge is a solution waiting to happen.

Consider thoughtfully and imaginatively and note down solutions to challenges that you have:

11. Booklover You

"Reading is to the mind what exercising is to the body."
Richard Steele – 16ᵗʰ and 17ᵗʰ Century Irish Writer and Politician

I like reading a lot. One minute you can be lying on a beach of white sand, the clear blue sea lapping at your feet, and the next standing in a spaceship orbiting Jupiter. You could be in the wild plains of Africa, wiping the sweat from your brow, or deep undersea amidst the dark blue water in a submersible. Words give you freedom, a sanctuary for your imagination with vistas for your mind to see.

If you prefer reading non-fiction then any area you are interested in is good as well. You might prefer reading autobiographies or biographies about people that you admire. It's also heartening to revisit childhood favourites and other books from your past.

Personally I do enjoy reading self-improvement books. I want to learn how to be a better me. I want to improve in the areas of my life that need improvement. I want to grow and progress and those types of books, such as this one, help you do that. Why wouldn't you want to be a better Superhuman You?

I read one that had in it a chapter called "Find Your Voice," so I did, stopped reading it, and wrote this self-help book.

You might prefer romance novels, action and suspense, political intrigue or humour. It's just important that you read, that you read every day or night, that you encounter many books and many different lives, tales and alternate perspectives. You can expand your experience greatly by simply reading words on a page, and turning from one page to the next.

When I was a toddler I had books read to me: "Winnie the Pooh", "The Wind in the Willows", "Thomas the Tank Engine" and many others.

When I was at infants' school I liked reading the "Mr Men" books, Dr Seuss stories, and we had books read to us as we sat in a group.

When I was at juniors' school I read books that I don't remember the name of now, but I still remember parts of them: a girl who went on adventures in a fantastical land; a weasel burned a book of magic in a fire; in another, characters had a code of putting words in reverse order when then spoke. At that time I also read Roald Dahl books like "George's Marvellous Medicine", "Fantastic Mr Fox" and "The Twits."

When I was at secondary school I was keen on reading the "The Hitchhiker's Guide to the Galaxy" series of books because they were very funny, had good ideas and characters in them. Another great book that I read was "The Neverending Story."

At school we read different poetry and books, and in the last couple of years the plays "An Inspector Calls" and "Romeo and Juliet" and the book "Of Mice and Men."

When I was at college I did English A-Level and we read the books of "The Great Gatsby", "Beloved" and the plays "Our Country's Good" and "A Winter's Tale" and the poetry of Keats, amongst others. On my own I read "I Know Why the Caged Bird Sings" and several more.

When I was at university I didn't read at all and this continued into adulthood until I went to an osteopath who inspired me to read books again. Every time I saw him he would say, "What are you reading? What are you reading?" That was enough to get me reading again so I had an answer to his question.

I decided to read some of the classics so over a period of time I read "Animal Farm", "Nineteen Eighty-Four", "Gulliver's Travels" and "Treasure Island." They were all well worth reading.

Books from the bestseller list are great as well so one that I read was "The Curious Incident of the Dog in the Night-Time," a clever and interesting book.

When I was unwell, a few years after my issues first began, it was then I started reading self-improvement books.

When I was a teacher I had a boy in my tutor group that needed to improve his English skills so I advised him that he should read more. The books he liked were about motorbike racing and football, and he enjoyed them and they would only do his mind good.

A Superhuman You needs to know that when you read, the words become your thoughts, so it is important that you read positive, uplifting and inspirational books, with a worthy philosophy and a good heart. Reading is thought. So make your thoughts good ones. Enjoy them and be fulfilled.

A Superhuman You is responsible for what you read and that you keep reading and learning from the ongoing experience, as Confucius, the ancient Chinese philosopher said, "You cannot open a book without learning something," a lifetime of learning and a long history of books that you've read that continues after childhood and school.

As a Superhuman You my only question to you is, after finishing this book, what are you reading?

Catalogue a collection of books that you would like to, and will, read:

12. Poster Display

"The aim of art is to represent not the outward appearance of things, but their inward significance."

Aristotle – Ancient Greek Philosopher and Polymath

As I mentioned before, I had a long period of being unwell, which affected my outlook on life in not a positive way. To pick up my spirits and turn my life around I set to creating an outward visual representation of how I wanted to feel.

This began with printing many different smiley face pictures that I found using Google images. I then put them up on my living room wall opposite my settee where I see them most of the time. I saw them as a new permanent feature. The constant, positive reinforcement of mainly yellow, smiley faces, and some other colours, was great and really did make me feel happier.

Next I put up pictures on the left-hand side wall of my living room. I am a very visual person and like colour, so they were of different types of rainbow and colour spectrum depictions. They were images that I would be glad to see up on my wall.

Then I began to think about who my heroes were, what I cared about, and what inspirational figures could be up on my wall to motivate me. I chose ones that were real and fictional, 6 of each. The real ones from the worlds of social change, sport and film, and the fictional ones from TV shows and films that I liked. For each one underneath I wrote their name then a sentence as to what they had achieved, what I admired about them, or a great quote that they said, or line written for their character. I could look up at it daily, and, in fact, many times a day, to get a mental and physical boost.

I put more posters across and above of my stairs and in my bedroom too. They had sentences relating to issues that I had and wanted to conquer. They began, "The balance of a...", "Still hands of a...", "Vocal talents of a..." and "Strong and Still." The idea of them was to create subliminal messages to my subconscious as to what I wanted to improve. They were visible reminders when I walked down the stairs and when I woke up in the morning.

After a while I added to the displays with extra motivational ones that I put in my spare bedroom. There were 6 more with names and a sentence below. On the other side of the room I made further "Energy of a...", "Strength of a..." type posters.

As well in my bedroom I put up a large montage of different images, several for each to express my many ambitions. There were no gaps between them, an interlocking display, white borders around the pictures as before this time creating a framework of white, joining the pictures together.

It may be that your choices, needs and what you are passionate about vary from me. It could be that printouts of works of art, paintings, your own photos, photos of family and friends, good times that you've had, would be more uplifting for you and better to display on the walls of your house.

If you can afford it pictures could be framed, maybe a qualification that you are proud of, and even paintings such as watercolours might be bought. There is a wealth of possibilities.

There are motivational posters that can be found on the internet, or bought in stores. Whatever it is, it should inspire you, motivate and stimulate.

This is the art of a Superhuman You.

Write down a list of subjects that you would like to put up on your walls:

13. Rainbow Outlook

"Train your brain to focus on the good in every situation."
Karen Salmansohn – 20th and 21st Century American Author, Columnist and Motivational Speaker

It's more than appreciating the fact that every cloud has a silver lining, it's more than seeing a glass as half full, it's about wholeheartedly looking and trying to find the positives. It may be raining but with the sunshine as well, there must be a rainbow somewhere, so why not try to find it?

I have learnt very powerfully through the events in my life how important it is to be positive. It affects your reality, your actions and your world. What you perceive as being true, for you, is. You have Superhuman eyes, ears and touch so that you can see, hear and feel how beautiful a place the Earth is, so use them.

I see my life through a positive filter, that's the mindset I have and what I live. For that reason I don't watch the news on TV or read any newspapers. If they reported about all the good events that happened in the world that day, all the great people and all the amazing acts they had performed, accounts that were inspiring and uplifting, then I would.

I like reading constructive books, watching television programmes with good intentions, listening to stimulating music and I feel a boost from watching a good film that I've enjoyed.

For every chapter in this book I found a positive quote that fitted its content. I wanted to begin, continue, and finish them in a worthwhile way.

Feel great.

Feel fantastic.

Then go out into the world as a Superhuman You with your Rainbow Outlook and find that your life is full of rainbows.

Note all the great aspects about your life and how you live it:

14. Sleep Easy

"A well-spent day brings happy sleep."
Leonardo Da Vinci – 15th Century Italian
Renaissance Polymath

I have had issues with being able to get to sleep and stay asleep at various times so I have learnt a lot of techniques to overcome the circumstances, so I will share them with you.

I make sure that my bedroom has a strong connection to going to sleep, so there is no TV or games console, and I don't read at night in bed. In fact, I have a wind-down period of two hours before going to bed where I am not on my laptop, doing exercise or getting mentally over stimulated.

I have an alarm clock/ radio which is easily my favourite method of being woken up: different every morning and music that I like. It made a slight noise so I moved it into the far corner of the room. I turned it sideways, so I still used it as an alarm, but couldn't read the time on it from my bed during any point through the night.

I bought a new, silent, digital clock to have at my bedside. When tapped it illuminates, so I can't see the time on that either unless I want to. There is no time when you sleep.

I am consistent when I go to bed each night and when I get up, making sure that I get a good amount of sleep. I usually stay in bed through the night until my alarm goes off in the morning to tell my mind and body that I want to be tired, inactive and asleep until I get up.

For several months I used a relaxation technique, which involved my version of a "staircase" thought process that I had heard on a couple of relaxation CDs. For instance, "I am standing at the top of a staircase, with steps that go downwards in front of me, and I know that the further I go down them the more tired I will become and I will go to sleep. I go down onto the first step and I feel extremely drowsy and heavy. I go down onto the second step and I feel even more sleepy and tired... I reach the bottom of the stairs and I feel incredibly heavy, extremely tired and massively drowsy and I am going to sleep."

Sometimes I only reached the second step before I went to sleep and other times I went through the whole of it twice, but it always worked. You can tell your brain how you want to feel, and do it with quiet, slow, relaxed thoughts.

After this I also went on to doing meditation during the day or during the late evening works really well. It is by far the best way I have found to get to sleep quickly and get back to sleep if I wake up during the night.

I sit in a quiet room with the TV off. I close my eyes and, with my mouth closed as well, I breathe in and out slowly through my nose. The intention then is to not think about anything and if thoughts do come into your head then you can let them drift away like leaves on running water. Or you can think slowly in time with your breath "in" and "out."

I began with 10 minutes a day and built up to 20. Later on I meditated a few times in the late evening for 5 minutes: it was practise for going to sleep, like warming up before you exercise.

A Superhuman You realises the importance of getting a good night's sleep and being refreshed from it. Sleep is the time when you recharge and as Mohandas Gandhi said, "…the next morning, when I wake up, I am reborn."

Document ways in which you can improve your sleeping habits:

15. Confident You

"No one can make you who you want to be, except you, yourself."
Alem Mumuni – 20th and 21st Century Ghanaian Paracyclist

Whereas courage is needed to overcome, confidence is more to do with progressing from that point to where you feel relaxed, strong, in control and good at what you are doing. In the same way as building up courage in a particular environment, confidence too can be increased gradually.

From being unwell I had issues with my confidence: wondering if people noticed my being unstill, having an unsteady balance or the unease I sometimes had in speaking. The secret for me was getting to the point that I didn't mind if they did or not. I was confident enough to walk around in public and talk to anyone.

Other aspects of concern also related to my interactions with people. So I worked on steps to progress and become better at it. The first step is eye contact. It is important to look people in the eye, to share a moment, and you can do it with family, friends and people at the till in shops. A brief look and a smile communicates your friendliness. It's about holding that gaze as well.

There's also body language, being open when you talk to people, being confident in the way you sit, stand or walk. A touch on someone's shoulder or arm can show affection and trust. What you do with your body conveys meaning and intent, and being positive with it can improve how you feel.

And there's your speaking voice. The fact that you can speak loudly enough to be heard and clearly enough to be understood, that you get your point across and you say what you want to say. You have a worthwhile contribution to make so make it. To connect with people through speech is very important. Talking brings people together.

Through all of these aspects it's about being congruent, conveying a singular message in every way that you are a confident person and that you live a confident life. You create the Superhuman You that you are.

Small details can increase your confidence with people. One of these is to include how you feel or think about something in your speech, being emotionally honest in a positive way can be liberating; and it is important to be able to respond in the moment and get the best out of yourself when interacting with others.

A major aspect in which I increased my confidence was in being at nightclubs and enjoying myself. The first time I went to one was when I was still at secondary school and about 15. I didn't dance and I didn't like it. I went to nightclubs a few times at university and that was quite good but it was only after university that I started to go to nightclubs a lot. I began to loosen up, value being there and dancing with my friends. It reached the point where I had the confidence to be on a podium dancing where everyone in the nightclub could see me. A nightclub became a place where I was confident, relaxed and it felt natural to be there.

I had an issue with being unable to show I was displeased with anyone and display that emotion to people, but actually it isn't a very productive emotion. It is much better to develop communication and understanding. Through that you can get an amicable, mutually beneficial solution. If it doesn't work at first then you have to keep trying. One device I used to speak to people I was displeased with was to visualize them as little children: in that way they had less power and I was the one in charge, then I could control the situation to resolve differences.

A concern with being able to show a woman I am attracted to her is a skill I keep working on all the time. My desired result is to show that I am interested, then if they are too, I ask them out and then we start dating. There are a number of techniques I use to increase my confidence. Showing you are interested in someone is as simple as looking and smiling at them for a couple of seconds so that they notice. It is then crucial to talk to them to begin a connection and relationship. You can improve your thoughts, rehearse and visualize successful outcomes and build experience by doing.

So, if courage is for overcoming, and confidence is building up beyond that, where a Superhuman You is self-assured, strong, relaxed and decides to react positively to a given set of circumstances, then that is the mindset to have.

Experience arises through repetition and it gives you the insight and instinct of likely outcomes in different settings. As well as that you can deal with the unexpected: the knowledge that you can cope with anything and not mind what anyone else thinks, that is the true self-belief of a secure Superhuman You.

You can become confident at everything you want to, a Superhuman You changes your state of mind and actions into positive and useful ones.

Think about and note what your own steps for building your confidence are:

16. Swimming Without Arms

"What we do inspires people to try that little bit harder, whether they are able-bodied or disabled."
Margaret McEleny – 20th and 21st Century Scottish Paralympic Swimmer and Swimming Coach

And so the Olympics happened in Britain. It was the 2012 London Olympics. It was a superb festival of sport, athletics, human endurance, excellence and achievement. It was a magnificent celebration.

After the initial Games were finished it was time for the Paralympics. Maybe it was because I lived in the country they were being held, maybe increasingly their profile had been raised over a number of years, maybe it was just their time, but the Paralympics seemed to be more prominent and visible than ever before.

I watched a lot of sports such as Sailing, Wheelchair Tennis, Judo, Cycling and the Athletics. Then, one morning, I watched the swimming and there were two men competing that had no arms: Zheng Tao from China and Iaroslav Semenenko of the Ukraine.

They, and 6 other competitors, were doing the men's 100 metre backstroke final, up and down, much faster than I could with two arms. It struck me that this was the literal embodiment of being Superhuman: performing acts that few would have thought possible and moreover being among the

49

best in the world at it, Zheng winning gold and getting the world record, and Iaroslav getting fourth.

The phrase "Superhuman" was used a lot in the commentary of various sports, and particularly by Adam Hills on the channel 4 TV show "The Last Leg" whose first series covered the 2012 Paralympic Games. From his frequent use of the term "Superhuman" and these Paralympic Games it was then that I had the idea for this book.

The incredible, inspiring competitors made me think about the fact that we all have the potential to be a Superhuman You just like they are, and just like you can be too.

Write a list of all the great accomplishments that you have achieved or made happen:

17. Disciplined You

"Discipline is the bridge between goals and accomplishment."
Jim Rohn – 20th Century American Entrepreneur, Author and Motivational Speaker

To live as well as I can despite M.S., I have to be disciplined. Every day before I get up I do exercises, then in the morning I read, workout and meditate. I also often have a shower, and sometimes a shave. It is the access point to my day.

I feel like it has been worthwhile already before it is even the afternoon, and I am energized to work and, as a bonus, I can get whatever else done as well, and maybe go out in the evening and be with friends.

Also I write each day: this book. I have to do it for no more than an hour at a time maybe twice a day if it's going well and I have no other distractions. It's about having the discipline to keep taking small, cumulative steps. You need to have the long game in mind.

There is an experiment where you put a sweet in front of a child and tell them that if they wait one minute before eating it then they will get another sweet. So it's a choice of one sweet now or two if you wait a minute. It examines whether a child is able to delay gratification or not, and there is evidence to suggest that children that are able to will lead more successful, productive and happy lives.

You have to see the worth of what you are doing even if results don't happen quickly. Structure provides you the set-up to achieve what you want; you can develop a framework that gives you the greatest chance possible.

I take tablets each day too and it is important that I take them on time. Everything I do is so that my health is as good as it can be. I go to bed and get up at a consistent time and give myself enough rest during the day. You find a structure that works for you, stick to it and accrue the benefits.

One of the best choices I ever made was to stop watching TV, or at least so much of it. There were times when all I could do was watch TV throughout the whole day but later on I had enough of it so I deleted all that I had saved on my Sky+ box, including the many series record links.

I then watched an hour for each meal: breakfast, lunch and tea; and at most 2 or 3 hours in the evening if I was in. I recorded less and stopped watching a lot of programmes. I realized it was preventing me from doing as much as I could each day and it was easier to when the television was turned off. I had more peace and quiet, and time and space, and that is the greatest gift you can give to yourself.

Being disciplined is as much about what you don't do as what you get done. Only do acts that are healthy for your mind and body. Each day should be lived to make yourself better and more able to achieve your goals, ranging from short to long term.

Habits and routines are the stepping-stones to maintain structure in your life. They need to be good and beneficial; you create them by considered thought so that you enable yourself to excel at whatever it is you want to do.

When you act towards your liberation your life will become much easier. You are working to promote what it is that you are, you have your own back, you are in your own corner, you can be your own greatest advocate, champion, exponent and guardian.

When I was growing up I had a computer game called "Subterrenea" on the Commodore 64. You were a spaceship shooting enemy craft in different caves. It could be loaded from a cassette tape that had other games on it, and this game was part of the way into the tape. Every time I set it to load I trusted that the previous time I had played the game I had rewound the tape to the correct place, using the counter on the cassette player, so that it went back to 000. In this way I never had to look for the start of the game on the tape and I made it easier for my future self.

That trust in myself I misplaced for a while, when I was a teenager and in my twenties, but when I rediscovered it, it meant that I became much happier and more successful in my life.

A Superhuman You puts in the effort to live a structured day; you are disciplined and can maintain doing little and often to move you towards your ambitions.

Minute, increasing stages are the approach that will get you to where you want to be. Vision, focus, conviction and belief in yourself and your abilities are the guiding principles on which a Superhuman You lives and thrives. Actions are for your own betterment and they are always in a useful direction. You give yourself purpose for what it is you want to do.

Note how you are going to be more disciplined so that you will improve your life:

18. The Placebo Effect

"If you put your mind to it you can accomplish anything."
Doc Brown/ Back to the Future – 20ᵗʰ Century American Film Character

The human mind is so powerful that whenever a new medicine is developed it has to be tested against the placebo effect: the amount that you will get better because your brain thinks that you are receiving a cure, although it is a placebo that has no inherent medical benefits. Medicines have to be better than your mind is at healing yourself.

The strength of the human mind is incredible. Once, when I was a teenager, I simply took a pencil out of a pencil case and I thought that the dark grey lead end was nearer to me, and so for a moment I saw it as being so. Then I realized the other end was pointing towards me. I actually saw what I wanted to see, what I expected to see. This can happen with sound, taste and touch as well, where it is possible to experience what you want to if you believe it strongly enough.

This awesome power to determine how you perceive the world around you is a skill that needs to be harnessed by a Superhuman You. The way in which I tapped into it was by doing "The Lightning Process" training programme. I learnt that M.E. was a collection of shortcuts that my brain had become very good at doing in response to disquiet even though it had long since passed and was no longer an issue.

I had a consistently unclear mind. I used "The Lightning Process" for it and it led me to the idea of visualizing a white healing droplet falling into a black pool of water, sending out ripples. The splash it causes creating many more white healing droplets to rise and fall and so on. I focused this on the parts of my head that were affected and it turned the sensation off. Over time I stopped the concern completely.

The first time I had M.S. nerve discomfort, the toes of my left foot had tenderness for a few days, and it was impairing my ability to walk. I resolved that I would never go through having a feeling like that again. M.S. means that some of the myelin sheathing covering the nerves is not there and so the brain gets a message that your body is having an unwanted experience. I decided to visualize double thickness myelin sheathing throughout my whole body covering my entire nervous system. When I get discomfort in a specific area, such as in my right hand, I look at and focus on that area, thinking about the double thickness myelin sheathing, stopping the unwanted message being sent to my brain. It shortened any sensation to a few seconds or at most a few minutes, and stopped it altogether most of the time.

There are Neuro-Linguistic Programming techniques that I have selected and simplified for myself into what works best for me. If I have seen an image that I don't like I imagine it becoming grey and fading into the distance. If I see a situation I like I imagine the picture of it getting brighter and bigger as it moves towards me. You can control how much a stimulus has an effect on you. If there is a topic that I don't want to be concerned about, I think, "Stop. Block it out. Not interested. Move on." Leaving me free to think about what I enjoy and that which makes me smile.

A Superhuman You has a Superhuman Mind that you are in control of. Whatever happens in your life you can control its affect on you, as Jacob says in the TV show "Lost", "You always have a choice."

Your mind is your salvation.

Detail when you have been in control of your mind and affected the outcome positively:

19. Adapt and Overcome

"There is no education like adversity."
Benjamin Disraeli – 19th Century British Prime Minister

This is one of the main, central tenants of my philosophy: it's the way life should be lived, enjoyed and embraced. For me, the idea of it developed out of necessity for the challenges I faced because of having M.E. and particularly M.S.

I had an issue with my left hand being unstill when I went to do an action, an intention tremor. It was made more significant by the fact that I was left-handed for most activities.

When I couldn't write anymore because my left hand was moving too much, I decided to become right-handed. I took a few pages of A4 lined paper and on the first I wrote lines of capital letters with my right hand. I went from A to Z filling up the page with hundreds of letters, doing a line of "A's" then a line of "B's" and so on. On the next piece of paper I wrote a side of lower case letters in the same way. Then on the last page I wrote lines of special characters: all the while practising dexterity and fine motor control of my right hand.

After that I had greater confidence and ability of writing right-handed and every time I wrote with my right hand, whenever I needed to, it was more practise for what I wanted to achieve. Soon enough it wasn't a concern at all and it just *was* the case that

I was right-handed for writing. I adapted and overcame. I did what I needed to, to fix the situation.

Other aspects of my right-handedness were using it to pick up objects, and that was a case of always remembering to use the correct hand. And if I had to use both hands to do an activity I pinned my left hand against my side so that it couldn't move. Even to type this book I have my left hand on my laptop, with the thumb tucked underneath to give some height and stability, and it covers a third of the keyboard's keys, and the right hand is more mobile and is used for two-thirds of the keyboard.

Eating became a one-handed affair, having only a fork in my right hand using it to pick up food. If I needed to cut something up I would use the side of my fork to press through it.

Then there's carrying water in a glass, my left hand does a large amount of being unstill and the water goes everywhere, and my right hand too is unstill a bit, so I developed a method of carrying a glass from above so it's more stable and movement happens less and has less effect.

Brushing my teeth I changed from a normal toothbrush to an electric one, to limit the amount of movement required by me. For shaving I changed from razors, where being unstill began to cause me issues, to an electric shaver that was safer and better to use, and later I found a make of razor that I was able to shave with properly. In relation to all of this my first step was changing from left to right-handed.

I started off with head movements as well, but medication helped with that and it was only a case of getting over the concern of others seeing it when it happened. Later on, after my right hand started to be unstill a little as well, I adapted my techniques and ways to overcome it further.

All of this took a while for me to work out but I did it in the end and I became adept at adapting: a useful skill to have.

In respect to my balance issues I lean back against a wall when I get dressed, or put my shoes or trainers on, so as to be stable. I am careful when walking and turning and take it slow. Going up and down stairs I used to put one hand on the rail and my other hand on the wall, taking the need away for me to balance at all. Later I realised it would be a better idea if I only had my right hand on the rail walking upstairs and my right hand on the wall walking downstairs. Using the stairs became a place for me have a stable, partially influenced, balance so that it was easier and more consistent elsewhere.

For this and for a hundred other matters I adapt and overcome. I learn and consistently improve on my knowledge and methods.

I know that I could have a lot more challenging factors to deal with: emotional, physical or mental; but whatever it is I know that it could be adapted to and overcome. Never giving up and fighting for what you want, even if it is the doing of small daily tasks, is a part of the human spirit.

My point is that as a Superhuman You, you can overcome any adversity, you can adapt to any environment, face any challenge and you can find a way to overcome it, and in the process of doing so you become a wiser, stronger, better, more aware and more evolved Superhuman You.

Note times you have adapted to and overcome issues that you have experienced:

20. Brilliant You

"We are the hero of our own story."
Mary McCarthy – 20th Century American
Author, Critic and Political Activist

You are brilliant: you matter; your life matters. You are the best possible version of yourself and yet you are still managing to improve daily.

You are fantastic: there is no one else like you because you are unique, one of a kind, special in every way. All the answers you will ever need in life exist within your own head, or if not, then you can make sure to find them.

You are wonderful: you make people happy with your presence and enrich the lives of others. You make a positive difference and you are significant to the people that you know, and those you meet as well.

You are beautiful: a wondrous creation; a marvel of the world; inside and out. Your soul and spirit are beautiful too. Your true self glows with kindness and warmth.

You are incredible: you can do whatever you set your mind to. You can achieve everything you want by believing in yourself and your ability to make positive differences to your life.

You are exceptional: a stunning combination of life and energy. You make the greatest value of your actions a reality, and garner the benefits. You make all events better with your grace and dignity.

You are amazing: the love you can give and receive is unbounded. You turn every environment into a positive one and get the best from all concerned. You make other people as happy and fulfilled as you are.

You are a Superhuman You.

Make a list of ten or more brilliant aspects about yourself:

21. Active Positive

"Give everything on every single point."
Andy Murray – 21st Century Scottish
Professional Tennis Player

When I saw a hypnotherapist who also did
Neuro-Linguistic Programming and Cognitive
Behavioural Therapy, during my conversations with
her, I learnt a very valuable lesson. It wasn't
enough to be positive; I had to do more with that
state of mind, make the most out of my positive
mindset. I had to be Active Positive.

It was then I started doing the daily exercise,
and I began to make myself fitter, which made me
able to do more each day and activities such as the
weekly shop were easier and quicker. I began also
to read every day, so that my mind was being
improved as well. Each of these actions had
positive knock-on effects to my health: mind and
body.

I took charge of my life so that I made the most
out of it. I had to be trying, striving to make it
better. If I had to do exercise each day, read, write,
eat and drink well, put posters on the wall to make
me happier and more inspired, change my
philosophy and approach, then I would do it.

In terms of work my ability of how many pupils
I could tutor increased, and I became busier and had
more to do each day, and helping students by doing
the job I was experienced and very good at meant
that I had higher self-esteem, more focus and drive,

and more belief in myself for the circumstances I had to overcome daily.

I saw that I should go out with friends and keep in touch with them so that there were opportunities to socialize and enjoy myself. It's great to have friends that you care about and they care about you. Seeing them often develops and sustains the friendship.

Then there are significant partners and family members that mean more to you than anyone else. They deserve the most time, care and affection. Positive actions towards them are out of love and those relationships will develop and grow too.

From the idea of being Active Positive, I had a greater congruence to my life. My thoughts, way of speaking, and most importantly my actions, were all the same, they were all congruent for my own benefit and for the benefit of others. Anything you want to improve you have to work on, and you have to put time, energy and effort into it.

When a Superhuman You has an Active Positive mindset you are proactive in the decision of what your life is and how you can make it become that. Take on the challenges, be greater and better than any endeavour, break through and conquer to find solutions.

Exercise, reading, eating and drinking well, being for yourself, making positive actions only, to enhance your life that's how a Superhuman You is. You create external and internal stimuli that will enable you for what you want, creating a successful environment where you are productive and you are able to enjoy yourself with what you do.

Superhuman You is committed to a better life, being a great producer and your own benefactor of all that you desire. Your actions now, decide your future and what it is. For that reason, a Superhuman You is consistently an Active Positive You.

Register how you can become more Active Positive in your own life:

22. ...Into Strengths

Alfred (to Bruce Wayne): Why do we fall, sir?
So that we can learn to pick ourselves up.
Batman Begins – 21st Century American Film

Being unwell for several years, having M.E. and then M.S. might seem as not being good, but it has actually given me far more than it has taken. I am better, stronger, more knowledgeable, more positive and more able to take on any other challenges that life has for me because of it.

The skills, techniques and mentalities I learnt have made my experience better than it would have been, and I wouldn't have gained those traits without going through the journey that I have.

I exercise every day; I enjoy it and I am fitter than with the amount I did before. I am very pleased that I have found a new way to regularly exercise and I have adapted from playing various sports to playing them on Xbox Kinect.

I read every day, more than I used to, and I mainly read self-improvement books so I am constantly learning and improving. There are books that I am glad that I have read that have added to my life greatly.

I started doing meditation and gained many advantages from that. I have a larger amount of focus, self-belief and purpose; it helps me sleep better too. I learnt much more about mental processes and how I could control my thoughts. I have empowered my brain to be what I want it to be, to give myself that which I need.

The M.E. brought about understanding that helped me with the M.S. and my life in general. "The Lightning Process" training programme; the sessions with the hypnotherapist who also did N.L.P. and C.B.T.; the skills and techniques: they are all a major part of my life that I live now.

I had to stop doing full-time teaching, but the tuition I do I really enjoy as well. It's easier, more relaxed, and through it I have continued to meet a lot more great and nice students and their parents. I have learnt more about my subject as well, so I am now a better tutor for it.

Also I gained knowledge of diaphragmatic breathing: moving your diaphragm rather than your chest to breathe. You push your stomach out to draw your breath in, and then you bring your stomach back in and it pushes your breath out. It can be done during the day and it can increase levels of calm, emotional balance and improve your health. This is Superhuman You breathing.

In addition my mentality had to change. I was already quite a positive person but I had to be more positive, only interested in the good in every happening, having a Rainbow Outlook, having a positive filter, always looking for solutions and being Active Positive with my life.

So I have become fitter, and do more exercise; I read a greater amount and have learnt much from it; I mediate, am better at using the power of my mind, am more positive and solution orientated, I often do diaphragmatic breathing and I know and can do much more than before I had become unwell, and all of my experiences and knowledge that I built up, led to me writing this book. In many ways being unwell is the best circumstance that ever happened to me.

You can always become better, stronger and wiser; you just have to make that a reality for yourself and your Superhuman You life. It is true that you are powerful beyond all measure, you decide how you behave and react to events and almost anything can be turned into a strength and a worthwhile experience. You just have to believe and work hard and fight and love.

So how do you change a situation into a positive one? How does an unease become a strength? You have to take ownership of what happens to you, face up to it. Then you make it into something valuable and meaningful to a Superhuman You.

Partly it is just thinking about what you have gotten from an unwanted occurrence, what you have gone through because of it, what of those instances is good and of benefit to you. Viewpoint affects matters greatly, and if you look at an event in the right way then you can see what you have learnt and accomplished because of it.

Turning your inabilities into strengths: that's what it's all about. You transform much of what happens to you into the positive, you control your own being for the betterment of yourself, people you interact with and know, and many people you haven't even met.

When, as a Superhuman You, you can turn your greatest issues into your greatest strengths then yours is the world.

Write what your greatest strengths can be in your life:

23. Abundance Mentality

"Abundance is not something we acquire. It is something we tune into."
Wayne Dyer – 20th and 21st Century American Author and Motivational Speaker

The opportunities in your life will be many. Whether it's in terms of your career, your personal relationships or your home. You will get lots of occasions to shine, to be your best possible self and to show that to other people.

In terms of your career you can find a new or different job if you want to. You need to work and get the education or training necessary so you can do one of the many diverse occupations out there. Or continue with your own job, enjoy it, and be the best at it that you can.

In terms of dating, there are likely to be thousands of individuals that you could go out with who would be suitable for you and you may have already met one of them and be in a relationship. Marriage, children, if you want that then you can go for it.

In terms of friends, if you make the effort and keep in contact with people, you will get invited out or you can ask if they will visit or want to do an activity with you. Shared hobbies are a good place to meet new people.

In terms of your home you can do anything you want with it that you can afford, live anywhere you desire to within your means. You make the most of your dwellings, and you decide its look and how it feels to you. Money can be spent on furniture or not if you want to spend it elsewhere.

The chances will be plentiful, as everything is an opportunity, but a Superhuman You has to treat each one as if it is precious: a gift to be treasured and respected. In that way, you make the most of the possibilities that present themselves to you. There is also the aspect that a Superhuman You acts to get more opportunities, and makes them occur, by giving them a chance to happen.

Record how you can make the opportunities you have more plentiful and act on them:

24. Lucky You

"Luck is where preparation meets opportunity."
Oprah Winfrey – 20th and 21st Century
American Talk Show Host, Actress and Producer

You make your own luck is a commonly used phrase that is true. Your beliefs about the world, your perspective, your opinions, how hard you work, how much effort you put into everything you do, how much you are on the search for good fortune: that's what decides how lucky you are.

Luck, often, isn't just an event that happens to you, it is something you enable. You bring about the situation that makes it more likely to take place.

When I was about 11 I watched an episode of Red Dwarf on television. The story was about luck and how you could inject yourself with some serum to make yourself extremely lucky. I believed in the idea that some of the time you could be luckier than others and you could make use of it. I took a card out of a deck trying to get an ace, then 3 more, trying to get the other aces to investigate how fortunate I was at any given moment. I kept repeating the experiment, replacing the cards in the deck after 4 picks. On one occasion I randomly selected 3 out of the 4 aces. The odds against me doing that were so high I considered myself to be very lucky and it was then I filled out a postcard with my address and name to enter a national competition to win a games console. Several weeks later I received a package. I opened it and on top there was a note saying "Congratulations! You're a winner!" And there was a Sega Master System inside: my first games console.

It could have been that judging my luck and writing the postcard when it was maximised had an affect on the outcome, but it was much more probable because of the fact I entered the competition about 10 times in all, and put drawings and lots of colourful shapes on a few of them, and the person picking out the winning entries may have noticed one of mine because of it.

Still, I like the idea that you have a fluctuating amount of luck, listen to it, make the most of any you have when it is high and you will benefit greatly. You have to be involved, you have to take your chances, you have to perform useful actions; but it is possible, and if you behave in the correct way: probable.

I was lucky that a friend of a relative had seen an article about "The Lightning Process" in a magazine, and the information was passed onto me. I was lucky that I met someone at university who I then had a long-term relationship with. I was lucky that I was a teacher, then tutor and am able to still do a job that I love. I was even lucky when a car crashed into the back of mine: I had a new, much better car from it, and a monetary settlement besides. I was lucky that I was unwell then had the idea for this book. Seemingly unfortunate luck can be seen as good from the right viewpoint.

A Superhuman You makes your own luck; you do all the setting up and work to make it be a reality and are on the lookout for it as almost any situation can be made into a good and lucky one.

As Thomas Jefferson said, "I'm a great believer in luck, and I find the harder I work, the more I have of it." So a Superhuman You has to take this deep into your Superhuman heart: you are lucky and that is how you make it that you will get all that you want.

Think and write about the many forms of good luck you have experienced:

25. Upward Spiral

"And he pushed them. And they flew."
Guillaume Apollinaire – 19th and 20th Century
French Poet, Novelist, Playwright and Art Critic

Something happens to you, something good, by design or by accident. It seems like an isolated incident at first but it leads on to something else that's good. The feelings of being positive and happy about your life increase a little.

You smile widely, possibly for the first time in days, weeks or even years. It is a wholehearted smile that comes from within and projects itself far beyond your body and into the world.

People notice your smile and it causes them to smile too. They want you to be around because they are better for you being there. Your presence is uplifting and you show glimpses of joy.

More good outcomes happen to you as a result of you being ready for them, you are prepared for all that is wonderful for you to experience. Feelings of bliss enter into your soul. When your life starts going well, it starts going really well. All the parts of your life are fitting into place and making sense.

You make the most out of the new environments you find yourself in and they lead to many more events that are great. The positive events multiply and keep happening to you. You are happier than you have ever been before.

You feel lighter; the amazing occurrences are pushing you upwards. Tremendous excitement in how fantastically everything is going for you gets you in an updraft of possibility. Your spirits and your body soar, you open your arms up to greet the fresh, inspiring light. You ascend towards what you could be. You are aloft of all that has happened to you before in your life, rising up beyond.

Can you feel your feet lifting from off the ground?

A Superhuman You finds yourself caught in an upward spiral and you have no reason but to fly.

Put what you can do to kickstart an upward spiral for yourself:

26. Change the World

Female Doctor: The world doesn't work this way.

Nathan Ford: So change the world.

Leverage – 21st Century American Television Show

If you want to change the world then first you have to change yourself. To change yourself is to change your life, your viewpoint and how you interact with everything and everyone around you. And that is what this book is all about.

If you have something good to put out into the world, if you have something worthwhile to say, if you can make a positive difference, then go for it with all your heart.

There are many ways in which I would like to change the world. I have dreams about the results I could engender with the ideas that I have that could really make a difference. Here are some of them:

I think that in an emergency room you should have a brief assessment by an experienced doctor at the point of entry, and you are put on a scale of 1 to 5: 5 being the highest and deserving of very serious, immediate attention; a 4: serious and seen within 10 minutes; a 3: quite serious and seen within 30 minutes; a 1 or 2: a minor complaint, you can be sent away, with perhaps a stitches-type plaster, a cleaned wound and some antiseptic put on. This would have stopped me waiting for hours a few times, when my wound was not long or deep enough to warrant stitches. It would mean a lot less waiting for people.

There should be a huge number of additional flowering trees, bushes and shrubs planted in towns and cities, and many more perennial flowers. It would make those places visually more appealing, raise people's sense of value in themselves and their environments and be better for bees and other pollinating insects.

In relation to this I had an idea called "The Million Trees Project." It would be about there being 1,000 more trees in 1,000 cities around the world. And at the start of each year the counter would be reset to 0. The priority would be to increase good, unpolluted air in built-up areas and make the cities more pleasant for the people living and working there. I have heard Central Park described as "the lungs of the city" for New York and every city should have the same number of trees and the same opportunity to be healthy and clean. Garden rooves would be work well too.

Solar panels should be on all houses and some vehicle rooves. New cars being made should all be electric or electricity/ petrol hybrids. A large proportion of the electricity made from solar, hydro and wind farms. Then from there they can progress to a point where cars run on hydrogen and the only exhaust product would be water. Charging points, in all petrol stations, would help for promoting electric cars. Every person making their way towards being self-sustaining in energy terms would be of great benefit to the world.

There should be TV programmes in every country that campaign for positive change and make those improvements happen. There should be many more programmes of the type that help people deserving of assistance in their lives; anything that makes a worthwhile difference.

There should also be news stations, papers and magazines that only report good news. It would make people feel happier about their lives and surroundings, you'd be able to see all about the brilliant people there are, the incredible feats they accomplish, everything that is great and everyone that is positive in their actions and mentalities. Let it be known how wonderful a world we live in and let us see it in all its splendour.

For countries that want to make their children and then adults more numerate, the first step would be to take all calculators out of the education system. There should not be any calculator test papers, instead students need to be well versed in their number work skills, learning times tables and other basics thoroughly at primary level, spending a week of every term in every year at secondary school, practising adding, subtracting, multiplying and dividing.

People often have lots of loose change in drawers, on trays, in bags or jars. All this money could be collected and given to charities. 1, 2 and 5p boxes would be put in banks and major supermarket chains, and schools collect from students the money that people don't want, that is inactive and unused. The lowest 3 denominations of any currency in every country could be collected from those that can afford to give it.

And change the world by writing this book.

Live a good life, help people, raise decent children, be good at your job, make meaningful connections with other people and leave the world a better place than how you found it.

Change the world one person at a time, change your life one important moment at a time and most crucially as Mohandas Gandhi rightly said, "Be the change that you wish to see in the world."

A Superhuman You is that change.

Inventory ways in which you can change your life and the world for the better:

27. Relentless You

"The most certain way to succeed is always to try just one more time."
Thomas Edison – 19th and 20th Century American Inventor and Businessman

You are climbing a mountain when you come across a wall of smooth, black stone extending upwards, vertically into the clouds, and left and right of you as far as you can see.

There is no way over or around it.

What do you do?

As a Superhuman You you realize that the wall is a manifestation of your own self-esteem, so you pick up your climbing equipment, take a deep breath, and walk straight through it.

You are always tenacious and keep fighting: there are no limits. The world is yours. You can be the person that you want to be, achieve what you want to achieve, live where your talents lie, and work there too.

I am constantly changing my approaches and solutions to issues that I have. The amount I read each day, the length of time I meditate for, the quantity of exercise I do, all vary and it relates to how much I need and how much I can make time for. I alter my ideas to suit my circumstances best, such as bringing diaphragmatic breathing and vocal practice, speaking to myself about anything for 20 minutes, into my morning routine. I am relentless in behaving in such a way so that I am able to live the most fulfilling life that I can.

That which you find not so easy you need to be the most relentless with: you only stop when you succeed. In life a Superhuman You expresses your opinions, wants to be and is, heard. You establish the boundaries for how people treat you in how you are to them. You set the agenda for each day and take responsibility for fulfilling all that you want to accomplish.

If you're not having a good day, week, year or life, you can decide to turn it around at any moment. You can get a lot done when you decide to take action and begin anew. If you need to make a fresh start you can have a reset to zero: cut your nails, shave and shower. Then you are ready to take on any challenge.

When people don't believe what you are capable of, or even you don't believe yourself that you can do something, it is important to remember the line shouted by John Locke in "Lost": "Don't tell me what I can't do!" I think this sentence a lot and it helps me to utilise every opportunity I encounter.

Despite what I have said in this chapter, sometimes you have to give yourself a break. You have to find humour in your blessings, take a light-hearted view of what happens to you and what you make happen; always allowing yourself to smile and laugh.

Also you have to know when your energies are best used somewhere else, when it is time to go another way. Sometimes you have to leave a situation, or person, alone and move on.

You can do anything. You can get everything you want. It is not an entitlement though, you have to prove yourself worthy, make the most of what you have, work hard, learn, develop and grow.

Having a Superhuman You will, you scale the mountain, one rise at a time.

And you always persevere.

Document parts of your life that you are going to be relentless with:

28. Other Reading

"Knowledge of what is possible is the beginning of happiness."
George Santayana – 19th and 20th Century
Spanish Philosopher, Essayist, Poet and Novelist

There are a number of self-improvement books that I have read, and many other sources from which I have learnt to overcome the issues I had first with M.E. and then M.S.

"The Lightning Process" training sessions, created by Phil Parker, were a superbly valuable experience: they gave me the understanding and tools to triumph over M.E. It is the starting point where I saw how fundamental it is to have a positive ethos, evidenced by the chapter, "Rainbow Outlook" and, in fact, this entire book. It enables and empowers the voice within you, the voice that says, "Stop!" to the unwanted and embraces and focuses on the good.

I have read several of his books and one that I would recommend is "The Ten Questions to Ask for Success." It was inspiring and motivating toward my goals. It had spaces where you could write comments and is the reason I have included written response sections in this book.

Next I read "Your Life Can Be Fantastic Too!" by Nik and Eva Speakman. This was a positive and uplifting work. It had pieces on various notable people called "Inspiring Lives" and it motivated me to do the idea I'd had for a while of putting A4 posters of my heroes up on my lounge wall, seen in the chapters "Hero Worship" and "Poster Display." There were quotes from them and many others, which inspired me to include quotes at the beginning of each of these chapters. It also has different techniques and mental exercises for you to try: workouts to improve your mind.

With the book there was a picture of them next to a flipchart with the phrase "Anything Is Possible" on it. I believe that to be true. I have placed it across from where I sit in my lounge, so that I can see it all the time, and think about its message.

Then I read "The 7 Habits of Highly Effective People" by Stephen R. Covey. I learnt a great deal from this book, and it inspired the chapters, "Interdependent You", "Mission Statement" and "Abundance Mentality." It continued to support and motivate me and gave me more tools and ideas from which I could build my character ethic, communication skills and approach for the undertaking of activities. It did make me a lot more effective in my daily life.

Now, as I write this, I am in the process of reading "Unlimited Power" by Tony Robbins. It is a brilliant book so far and if I had read it sooner it would have inspired chapters on "states" and "modelling": the concept of being able to decide the state you are in so you are at your most resourceful, and how to model successful peoples' attitudes and behaviours to get the same kind of results as they do.

There is much more I have yet to read and I am excited by the prospect of learning more techniques and mental processes to improve my world and how I approach it.

Books can be found in any area that you need help with so I encourage Superhuman You to go look for them, and find the ones that you think are great and useful to you and your life. And, actually, I was improved by them for much more than the reasons I bought them: I became more confident, stronger, had a higher sense of self-worth, was more aware of possibility and more productive.

Aside from the written word I learnt a great deal from the osteopaths, physiotherapist and speech therapists that I saw. I learnt how to look after myself, build a program of exercises and take care of and make it easier to use my voice.

The hypnotherapist who also did Neuro-Linguistic Programming and Cognitive Behavioural Therapy was very influential to me. She helped me overcome the psychological issues of M.S. before I knew what it was. She inspired the chapter "Active Positive" and therefore everything that arose from that approach, even perhaps, again, the writing of this book.

A Superhuman You is always striving to improve. You want to get better results, live a better life and be stronger and more empowered. There are many sources from which you can find answers, and as a Superhuman You, you handle them with ease.

There is excellence in the journey of self-improvement, you become wiser with each intelligent sentence you read, more aware with each enlightening idea you find, more proficient with each constructive action you are enabled to take.

Knowledge is your paradise.

Note what sources you can learn from and continue to improve:

29. Endings

"Change is the end result of all true learning."
Leo Buscaglia – 20th Century American
Professor, Author and Motivational Speaker

You are nearly at the end of the journey you have been on whilst reading this book. You can now look back on how far you have come. The Superhuman You parts of your character have been given life and sparkle brightly in you aura.

When I reached the last of the sessions I had with my hypnotherapist I thanked her for helping me to feel better by improving my outlook, she said "I gave you the tools, but you're the one who ran with it." So I'm asking you, as a Superhuman You, to run with it with all your might.

I can present my ideas; give you my thoughts on life shaped by all that I have been through when being unwell, and quote from the wisdom of others, but it is you that has to do something with the ideas, concepts and strategies. You have to be emotionally brave, make the most of what you have, make your experience of the world as good as you can, and help others to create their best possible lives too.

Your Superhuman Heart gives you the compassion to sense other people's emotions and know your own. Your Superhuman Mind allows you to perceive your surroundings accurately so that you master them confidently. Your Superhuman Body lets you interact physically with every environment healthily and with strength. Your Superhuman Sight, Hearing and Touch means that you see, hear and feel everything around you and its beauty fills you with awe. Your Superhuman Will means you have the courage to act, persevere or move on, always looking forward.

The most important aspect to remember though is what you are. You are a Superhuman You: we all have the capability for being Superhuman. So go for it, do it now, make your life great.

Write down the character attributes that you know that you now are:

30. Conclusion

"We are all Superhuman, we all have glorious powers and fantastic abilities deep within our heart, mind and soul, especially You."
Simon Sly – 21st Century English Author, Teacher and Tutor

Superhumans walk among us.

They are not always easy to see, as they bear no distinguishing features, no mark or sign on their skin or clothes. No affectations about their person to reveal who they are.

They could be the young man with glasses on his face, brown hair, that you pass in the street, an elderly woman going home with her shopping in her trolley she pulls behind her, a little girl happily playing and skipping with her friends, a teenaged couple holding hands and looking in a shop window for an engagement ring that they might buy, a more mature husband and wife driving along the road to get to a friend's house.

A Superhuman could be any one of these people: unbeknownst to you. You may though detect a glimmer of their true nature in the way that they smile at a stranger, thank a person for a small courtesy, be accepting of a minor infringement upon their person such as being bumped into or mistaken for another. These are their marks and signs.

Superhuman people inhabit the Earth, a planet like no other. They are capable of such strength, warmth, courage and charity. They number in their millions most not even aware of their own true power.

You arrive home, maybe after a hard day's work, maybe during a day relaxing and being with your family, maybe after being at a friend's or being with friends. You climb the stairs, or walk through the ground floor, and go into a bathroom. You look into the mirror and see a flash of something otherworldly, something magical, something brilliant. Then you have the greatest realization that you are Superhuman too. You are one of them. It was right there before you all along.

You see the cape around your shoulders, feel the boots on your feet, sense the strength in your body and mind, you can do anything, your potential is infinite, your life fated to be great in whatever way you choose it to be: helping others and living a good life, protecting and saving your part of the world on a daily basis, fighting for what you believe in, for the benefit of others and yourself.

The Superhuman trait is in you, craving to liberate itself: so that you can fulfill your destiny. It is waiting for you out there; it is waiting for you to complete the journey you have been on whilst reading this book. You can achieve and be and overcome whatever you want.

There are so many great people who have achieved so many great accomplishments, most of whom you wouldn't even know the name of: the Superhuman Masses. People that rise beyond their situations and surpass their challenges either mental or physical, either slight or not, and become the great heroes that the world wants them to be and that they deserve to be.

You too could rank among them.

Will you accept the call to be Superhuman?

Make a list of what Superhuman You has learnt from reading and writing in this book:

Top Ten Unused Quotes

"Peace begins with a smile."
Mother Teresa
20th Century Albanian-Indian Nun and Missionary

"Do good things and good things will happen."
21st Century American TV Sitcom Character
Earl Hickey/ My Name is Earl

"The purpose of our lives is to be happy."
Dalai Lama
20th and 21st Century Spiritual Leader

"The mind is everything. What you think you become."
Siddhartha Gautama "Buddha"
Ancient Indian Founder of Buddhism

"Fun is good."
Dr. Seuss
20th Century American Children's Author

Rainbow Quotes

"There's a rainbow in the sky all the time."
Ziggy Marley
20th and 21st Century Jamaican Musician

"May your journey through life be vibrant and full
of colorful rainbow
Harley King
20th and 21st Century American Writer

"My heart leaps up when I behold a rainbow in the
sky."
William Wordsworth
18th and 19th Century English Writer

"Be a rainbow in someone else's cloud."
Maya Angelou
20th and 21st Century American Writer

"Everyone wants happiness. No one wants pain.
But you can't have a rainbow, without a little rain."
Zion Lee
20th and 21st Century American Stuntman

"Keep looking up, there may be a rainbow waiting
for you."
Anonymous

"Please, Rainbow, give me another chance."
Anonymous

Paralympic Athletes of 2012

The London 2012 Paralympic Games were the biggest so far. There were many brilliant achievements of the Superhumans, here are some from Team GB:

Hannah Cockcroft, who started wheelchair racing when she was at university in 2007, won her events of 100m and 200m, beating the previous Paralympic records.

Ellie Simmonds, with a small stature and at the age of 17, defended her 400m Freestyle swimming title beating it by 5 seconds and won the 200m Individual Medley.

Sarah Storey had switched from swimming to cycling 10 years before and won gold in the Individual Pursuit, the 500m Time Trial and the Individual Road Race.

Jonnie Peacock ran, wearing a blade, to win the 100m amputee race at the age of 19, beating both the defending and world champions, in a record time of 10.85 seconds.

There are a great deal more medal winners and other amazing athletes that took part from the rest of the GB team, all of whom are incredible.

In the rest of Europe there were still further
incredible medal winners and competitors:

Esther Vergeer, from the Netherlands, won the
individual and doubles wheelchair tennis titles,
and was the most dominant player in Paralympic
sport.

Former Formula 1 driver Alessandro Zanardi,
from Italy, after losing both his legs in a crash,
won both the Road Time Trial and Road Race in
hand cycling.

After getting 3 silvers in swimming and 2
bronzes, Teresa Perales of Spain, in her last race
won the 100 Freestyle, the gold she has wanted
all along.

Germany's men's Sitting Volleyball team won a
bronze medal having only been ranked 8 out of
10, and not making it to the previous
Paralympics.

With seconds left on the clock Grigorios
Polychronidis, from Greece, threw a perfect shot
in the fourth round of the pairs final to win a gold
medal in Para Boccia.

Those and many other remarkable medal winners
and competitors took part from Europe.

In the rest of the world there are yet more wonderful athletes, here are some of them:

Zheng Tao the "armless swimmer" from China, won a gold medal in the 100m backstroke during his debut in the London 2012 Paralympics.

American Matt Stutzman, known as the "Armless Archer," became a London icon by winning silver in Archery and was an inspiration to many.

Jacqueline Freney, the swimmer from Australia, won 8 gold medals including the 100m Backstroke, 50m Butterfly and the 50, 100m and 400m Freestyle events.

The Rwanda men's Sitting Volleyball team didn't win any medals but they arose from the ashes of conflict and became the first team to qualify from their nation.

Brazil's Alan Fonteles Oliveira produced the biggest upset and shock in the stadium to win the 200m race. He is a double amputee below the knees.

Yohansson Nascimento, also of Brazil, a double arm amputee, won first a gold and silver, but had to hobble to the finish in the 200m after getting an injury.

The Israeli, Noam Gershony, survived an army helicopter crash just six years before the games, and went on to win a gold in Wheelchair tennis.

The Namibian Johanna Benson, who won gold in the 200m, was the first person of her country to win gold at any games, Paralympic or else.

Korea's Gwang-Geun Choi, wasn't even expecting to be on the judo podium, two weeks after getting out of hospital, but he came away with gold,

Another Brazilian, Jeferson Goncalves, scored half of the goals to lead their 5-a-side blind team to their third consecutive title, drawing or winning every game.

Four Australian women won the 4x100m Medley Relay in swimming by only 3 hundredths of a second, after being in 3rd or 4th place for half of the relay.

Abdullah Alary, from the United Arab Emirates, having not qualified for the previous Paralympics, won gold in the 50m rifle, only the second for his country.

Canadian, Patrick Anderson, won gold with his team in Wheelchair Basketball, having played in 4 Paralympic games, he scored a career-high number of points.

America's Jeremy Campbell, in addition to defending and winning the gold at the Discuss, broke the World Record 4 times.

Australian Swimmer, Matt Cowdrey, won 8 medals, 5 gold, to become his country's most decorated Paralympian of all time.

Earthquake survivor, Haitian Gaysli Leon, showed that even with suffering a spinal injury, he could still compete in Handcycling.

Fatma Omar, from Egypt, won gold in the Powerlifting competition and it was her fourth successive win in the Paralympics.

In his first year rowing internationally, Cheng Huang from China, claimed gold in the men's single Sculls in a record time.

Russia's Eduard Romanov scored a golden goal in the final to win his country's first football 7-a-side gold medal since 2000.

All of the medal winners and competitors are Superhumans for the challenges they overcome. They motivate the idea that it is possible to reach beyond your limits. They inspire everyone: future Paralympic athletes, anyone with a disability, and all people that watch or hear about them that can find it within themselves to be Superhumans like they are.

Printed in Great Britain
by Amazon